ONE QUESTION A DAY

A YEAR-LONG JOURNAL FOR KIDS

365 QUESTIONS TO ASK YOURSELF

A DAILY JOURNAL OF SELF-DISCOVERY

THIS BOOK BELONGS TO:

D1509579

Copyright Busy Kid Press. All rights reserved.

HOW TO USE THIS JOURNAL:

Congratulations on your new journal! This daily journal includes 365 fun and thoughtful questions — one for each day of the year. Do you want to get to know yourself a little better? Be sure to answer a question each day and you can look back after a year at all your amazing answers! Each date line is blank, so be sure to write in each day's date. That way, you can start on page one, no matter when you get started! This is a no-fuss journal. You have a few lines to write an answer, so don't feel like you have to write a lot. The thing to focus on is your consistency!

A journal is a special place just for you to be alone with your thoughts. The questions you'll find inside this journal are kid-friendly, and they are meant to help you discover yourself as a person. Remember, there is only one you, and you are very important.

We hope this journal becomes a keepsake for you to look back on when you're older. It will be interesting to do so!

JOURNAL TIPS:

- **Give your journal a special spot.** Maybe it's in a drawer, or under your pillow, or on your desk.

- **Pick a time of day you like to write in your journal.** Maybe it's before bedtime, or maybe it's first thing in the morning.

- **Don't worry about how you write!** It's more important to get out your thoughts — you don't have to be perfect! Your writing will improve each day.

- **Most of all, have fun!**

DAY 1 ♥   **DATE:** _____

What three words describe you best?

_____

_____

_____

_____

_____

─★─★─★─★─★─★

DAY 2   **DATE:** _____

Who is one person you look up to and why?

_____

_____

_____

_____

_____

─♥─♥─♥─♥─♥─♥

DAY 3   **DATE:** _____

If you could have any super-power, what would it be?

_____

_____

_____

_____

_____

_____

DAY 4 ♥   **DATE:** _____

What are two things you are grateful for?

_____

_____

_____

_____

_____

—★ —★ —★ —★ —★ —★

DAY 5   **DATE:** _____

What is your favorite memory?

_____

_____

_____

_____

_____

—♥ —♥ —♥ —♥ —♥ —♥

DAY 6   **DATE:** _____

If you could have any pet, what would it be?

_____

_____

_____

_____

_____

DAY 7 ♥   DATE: _____

What is your favorite thing to do for fun?

_____
_____
_____
_____
_____

—★ —★ —★ —★ —★ —★

DAY 8   DATE: _____

What magical creature would you want to meet?

_____
_____
_____
_____
_____

—♥—♥—♥—♥—♥—♥

DAY 9   DATE: _____

What's one thing that always makes you laugh?

_____
_____
_____
_____
_____

DAY 10 ♥

DATE: _____

What is your favorite subject in school?

_____

_____

_____

_____

_____

— ★ — ★ — ★ — ★ — ★ — ★

DAY 11

DATE: _____

Write a funny knock-knock joke below.

_____

_____

_____

_____

_____

— ♥ — ♥ — ♥ — ♥ — ♥ — ♥

DAY 12

DATE: _____

If you had a time machine, where would you go?

_____

_____

_____

_____

_____

_____

DAY 13 ♥︎   **DATE:** _____

What do you think the coolest job would be?

_____

_____

_____

_____

_____

—★—★—★—★—★—★

DAY 14   **DATE:** _____

Look out the closest window. What do you see?

_____

_____

_____

_____

_____

—♥—♥—♥—♥—♥—♥

DAY 15   **DATE:** _____

When you get angry, what helps to calm you down?

_____

_____

_____

_____

_____

_____

DAY 16 ♥   DATE: _____

What's the best advice someone has given you?

_____

_____

_____

_____

_____

—★—★—★—★—★—★

DAY 17   DATE: _____

What is one of your funniest memories?

_____

_____

_____

_____

_____

—♥—♥—♥—♥—♥—♥

DAY 18   DATE: _____

What do you love most about your family?

_____

_____

_____

_____

_____

DAY 19 ♥   DATE: _____

If you were a cartoon character, who would it be?

_____

_____

_____

_____

_____

—★—★—★—★—★—★

DAY 20   DATE: _____

What is your favorite color? What is your second favorite?

_____

_____

_____

_____

_____

—♥—♥—♥—♥—♥—♥

DAY 21   DATE: _____

What is the best way to spend a rainy day?

_____

_____

_____

_____

_____

DAY 22 ♥   **DATE:** _____

What talent or skill do you wish you had?

_____

_____

_____

_____

_____

—★—★—★—★—★—★

DAY 23   **DATE:** _____

Describe the perfect vacation.

_____

_____

_____

_____

_____

—♥—♥—♥—♥—♥—♥

DAY 24   **DATE:** _____

Which room in your house is your favorite? Why?

_____

_____

_____

_____

_____

_____

DAY 25 🖤   **DATE:** _____

What's your favorite holiday? Why?

_____

_____

_____

_____

_____

—★—★—★—★—★—★

DAY 26   **DATE:** _____

What makes a good friend? Who is your best friend?

_____

_____

_____

_____

_____

—♥—♥—♥—♥—♥—♥

DAY 27   **DATE:** _____

What makes you smile the most?

_____

_____

_____

_____

_____

_____

DAY 28 🖤   **DATE:** _____

Who is your hero? Why?

_____

_____

_____

_____

_____

—★—★—★—★—★—★

DAY 29   **DATE:** _____

If you could set a world record, what would it be?

_____

_____

_____

_____

_____

—♥—♥—♥—♥—♥—♥

DAY 30   **DATE:** _____

What is your greatest wish?

_____

_____

_____

_____

_____

_____

DAY 31 ♥   **DATE:** _____

If you could visit anywhere in the world, where would it be?

_____

_____

_____

_____

_____

—★—★—★—★—★—★

DAY 32   **DATE:** _____

What was your favorite toy when you were little?

_____

_____

_____

_____

_____

—♥—♥—♥—♥—♥—♥

DAY 33   **DATE:** _____

What is the most special/valuable thing you own?

_____

_____

_____

_____

_____

_____

DAY 34 🖤   **DATE:** _____

What is the best party you ever attended?

_____

_____

_____

_____

_____

—★—★—★—★—★—★

DAY 35   **DATE:** _____

If you had one-million dollars, what would you buy?

_____

_____

_____

_____

_____

—♥—♥—♥—♥—♥—♥

DAY 36   **DATE:** _____

Write about 2 places you'd like to visit someday.

_____

_____

_____

_____

_____

_____

DAY 37 ♥   **DATE:** _____

What are 2 of your favorite animals?

_____
_____
_____
_____
_____

—★—★—★—★—★—★

DAY 38   **DATE:** _____

If a genie granted you 3 wishes, what would they be?

_____
_____
_____
_____
_____

—♥—♥—♥—♥—♥—♥

DAY 39   **DATE:** _____

If you had to switch lives with someone, who would it be?

_____
_____
_____
_____
_____
_____

DAY 40 💜   **DATE:** _____

What is your favorite movie?

_____

_____

_____

_____

_____

—★ —★ —★ —★ —★ —★

DAY 41   **DATE:** _____

Write about your greatest strengths.

_____

_____

_____

_____

_____

—♥ —♥ —♥ —♥ —♥ —♥

DAY 42   **DATE:** _____

Write a note to your future grown-up self.

_____

_____

_____

_____

_____

_____

DAY 43 ♥   **DATE:** _____

What is your favorite month of the year? Why?

_____

_____

_____

_____

_____

—★—★—★—★—★—★

DAY 44   **DATE:** _____

What is something that worries you? Why?

_____

_____

_____

_____

_____

—♥—♥—♥—♥—♥—♥

DAY 45   **DATE:** _____

What is your favorite thing about yourself?

_____

_____

_____

_____

_____

DAY 46 ♥   DATE: _____

If you could be any animal, what would it be?

_____
_____
_____
_____
_____

—★—★—★—★—★—★

DAY 47   DATE: _____

What is your favorite game to play?

_____
_____
_____
_____
_____

—♥—♥—♥—♥—♥—♥

DAY 48   DATE: _____

What is the hardest thing about being your age?

_____
_____
_____
_____
_____

DAY 49 ♥︎   **DATE:** _____

If you had to change your name, what would it be?

_____

_____

_____

_____

_____

— ★ — ★ — ★ — ★ — ★ — ★

DAY 50   **DATE:** _____

Name 3 of your favorite things that are yellow.

_____

_____

_____

_____

_____

— ♥ — ♥ — ♥ — ♥ — ♥ — ♥

DAY 51   **DATE:** _____

Write about a place that's important to you.

_____

_____

_____

_____

_____

_____

DAY 52 ♥   DATE: _____

Describe a mistake you made that you learned from.

_____

_____

_____

_____

_____

—★—★—★—★—★—★

DAY 53   DATE: _____

The most interesting thing you've learned this year is...

_____

_____

_____

_____

_____

—♥—♥—♥—♥—♥—♥

DAY 54   DATE: _____

If you could invent anything, what would it be?

_____

_____

_____

_____

_____

_____

DAY 55 ♥   **DATE:** _____

If you could only eat one food all year, what would it be?

_____

_____

_____

_____

_____

—★—★—★—★—★—★

DAY 56   **DATE:** _____

If you could have any job in the world, it would be...

_____

_____

_____

_____

_____

—♥—♥—♥—♥—♥—♥

DAY 57   **DATE:** _____

What is one thing you want to accomplish this year?

_____

_____

_____

_____

_____

_____

DAY 58 💙   **DATE:** _____

Write a thank you note to someone you love.

_____

_____

_____

_____

_____

—★—★—★—★—★—★

DAY 59   **DATE:** _____

If you could change one thing in the world, it would be...

_____

_____

_____

_____

_____

—♥—♥—♥—♥—♥—♥

DAY 60   **DATE:** _____

You've sprouted wings! Where would you fly?

_____

_____

_____

_____

_____

_____

DAY 61 ♥   DATE: _____

What would be in your dream bedroom?

_____

_____

_____

_____

_____

—★—★—★—★—★—★

DAY 62   DATE: _____

Write about your favorite amusement park ride.

_____

_____

_____

_____

_____

—♥—♥—♥—♥—♥—♥

DAY 63   DATE: _____

What is the best gift you could ever get?

_____

_____

_____

_____

_____

DAY 64 ♥   **DATE:** _____

How did your parents choose your name?

_____

_____

_____

_____

_____

—★—★—★—★—★—★

DAY 65   **DATE:** _____

What does it mean to be

_____

_____

_____

_____

_____

—♥—♥—♥—♥—♥—♥

DAY 66   **DATE:** _____

Would you rather be very smart of very beautiful?

_____

_____

_____

_____

_____

_____

DAY 67 ♥   **DATE:** _____

What is your earliest memory?

_____

_____

_____

_____

_____

— ★ — ★ — ★ — ★ — ★ — ★

DAY 68   **DATE:** _____

What is the best thing to do on a snow day?

_____

_____

_____

_____

_____

— ♥ — ♥ — ♥ — ♥ — ♥ — ♥

DAY 69   **DATE:** _____

What is the most fun you've ever had with a friend?

_____

_____

_____

_____

_____

_____

DAY 70 ♥   DATE: _____

Describe the perfect weekend!

_____

_____

_____

_____

_____

— ★ — ★ — ★ — ★ — ★ — ★

DAY 71   DATE: _____

Did you try something new recently?

_____

_____

_____

_____

_____

— ♥ — ♥ — ♥ — ♥ — ♥ — ♥

DAY 72   DATE: _____

What do you feel is your greatest weakness?

_____

_____

_____

_____

_____

DAY 73 ♥   **DATE:** _____

If you were a Disney Prince/Princess, who would you be?

_____

_____

_____

_____

_____

—★—★—★—★—★—★

DAY 74   **DATE:** _____

Do you believe in yourself? Explain.

_____

_____

_____

_____

_____

—♥—♥—♥—♥—♥—♥

DAY 75   **DATE:** _____

Do you feel you are sometimes too hard on yourself?

_____

_____

_____

_____

_____

DAY 76 ♥   **DATE:** _____

What will you miss about school after you graduate?

_____

_____

_____

_____

_____

–★–★–★–★–★–★

DAY 77   **DATE:** _____

What do you do to relax?

_____

_____

_____

_____

_____

–♥–♥–♥–♥–♥–♥

DAY 78   **DATE:** _____

What did you laugh about recently?

_____

_____

_____

_____

_____

_____

DAY 79 ♥   DATE: _____

What is something you want to improve about yourself?

_____
_____
_____
_____
_____

— ★ — ★ — ★ — ★ — ★ — ★

DAY 80   DATE: _____

If you could learn any language, what would it be?

_____
_____
_____
_____
_____

— ♥ — ♥ — ♥ — ♥ — ♥ — ♥

DAY 81   DATE: _____

Who is the last person that made you laugh? Why?

_____
_____
_____
_____
_____
_____

DAY 82 ♥   **DATE:** _____

What are you most proud of?

_____

_____

_____

_____

_____

—★—★—★—★—★—★

DAY 83   **DATE:** _____

Describe an adventure you'd like to have.

_____

_____

_____

_____

_____

—♥—♥—♥—♥—♥—♥

DAY 84   **DATE:** _____

If you could live anywhere in the world, where would it be?

_____

_____

_____

_____

_____

DAY 85 🖤   **DATE:** _____

What is your favorite place to read or write?

_____
_____
_____
_____
_____

—★—★—★—★—★—★

DAY 86   **DATE:** _____

Finish this: When I'm an adult, I want to...

_____
_____
_____
_____
_____

—♥—♥—♥—♥—♥—♥

DAY 87   **DATE:** _____

What is your favorite snack or junk food?

_____
_____
_____
_____
_____

DAY 88 🖤   **DATE:** _____

Do you collect things? If not, what would you start with?

_____

_____

_____

_____

_____

—★—★—★—★—★—★

DAY 89   **DATE:** _____

Would you rather it always rain or always snow?

_____

_____

_____

_____

_____

—♥—♥—♥—♥—♥—♥

DAY 90   **DATE:** _____

Write a story in 25 words or less.

_____

_____

_____

_____

_____

DAY 91 ♥   DATE: _____

Write a poem about the color blue.

_____

_____

_____

_____

_____

—★ —★ —★ —★ —★ —★

DAY 92   DATE: _____

Write about the best surprise you ever got.

_____

_____

_____

_____

_____

—♥ —♥ —♥ —♥ —♥ —♥

DAY 93   DATE: _____

Write about a family tradition.

_____

_____

_____

_____

_____

_____

DAY 94 ♥   DATE: _____

Write about a time you were disappointed.

_____

_____

_____

_____

_____

—★—★—★—★—★—★

DAY 95   DATE: _____

What person in your life makes you feel confident?

_____

_____

_____

_____

_____

—♥—♥—♥—♥—♥—♥

DAY 96   DATE: _____

What would make an awesome treehouse?

_____

_____

_____

_____

_____

DAY 97 ♥   DATE: _____

What is your favorite day of the week? Why?

_____

_____

_____

_____

_____

—★—★—★—★—★—★

DAY 98   DATE: _____

If you could visit any planet, which one would it be?

_____

_____

_____

_____

_____

—♥—♥—♥—♥—♥—♥

DAY 99   DATE: _____

Describe the best field trip you've ever been on.

_____

_____

_____

_____

_____

_____

DAY 100 ♥   DATE: _____

Name five things you're good at.

_____

_____

_____

_____

_____

–★–★–★–★–★–★

DAY 101   DATE: _____

Describe your grandmother or grandfather.

_____

_____

_____

_____

_____

–♥–♥–♥–♥–♥–♥

DAY 102   DATE: _____

Who is your favorite book character?

_____

_____

_____

_____

_____

DAY 103 ♥   DATE: _____

What is something that makes you unique?

_____

_____

_____

_____

_____

—★—★—★—★—★—★

DAY 104   DATE: _____

If you were Queen/King for the day, what would you do?

_____

_____

_____

_____

_____

—♥—♥—♥—♥—♥—♥

DAY 105   DATE: _____

Describe something nice someone did for you.

_____

_____

_____

_____

_____

_____

DAY 106 ♥   **DATE:** _____

Describe your favorite vacation and why you enjoyed it.

_____

_____

_____

_____

_____

—★—★—★—★—★—★

DAY 107   **DATE:** _____

If you could be famous for something, what would it be?

_____

_____

_____

_____

_____

—♥—♥—♥—♥—♥—♥

DAY 108   **DATE:** _____

What do you think will be different about life in 2200?

_____

_____

_____

_____

_____

_____

DAY 109 ♥   DATE: _____

What is your biggest goal in life?

_____

_____

_____

_____

_____

—★—★—★—★—★—★

DAY 110   DATE: _____

What was the most embarrassing moment for you?

_____

_____

_____

_____

_____

—♥—♥—♥—♥—♥—♥

DAY 111   DATE: _____

Describe a rule you broke and why you broke it.

_____

_____

_____

_____

_____

_____

DAY 112 ♥   **DATE:** _____

What's one of the best decisions you've ever made?

_____

_____

_____

_____

_____

—★—★—★—★—★—★

DAY 113   **DATE:** _____

What is one of the worst decisions you've ever made?

_____

_____

_____

_____

_____

—♥—♥—♥—♥—♥—♥

DAY 114   **DATE:** _____

What do you find annoying? Why?

_____

_____

_____

_____

_____

DAY 115 ♥   **DATE:** _____

Write a note to yourself in 20 years from now.

_____

_____

_____

_____

_____

— ★ — ★ — ★ — ★ — ★ — ★

DAY 116   **DATE:** _____

What do you appreciate most about your parents?

_____

_____

_____

_____

_____

— ♥ — ♥ — ♥ — ♥ — ♥ — ♥

DAY 117   **DATE:** _____

What could you do to make the world a better place?

_____

_____

_____

_____

_____

DAY 118 ♥   **DATE:** _____

Write a bucket list of 5 things you'd like to do.

_____

_____

_____

_____

_____

—★—★—★—★—★—★

DAY 119   **DATE:** _____

What is your favorite sport? Why?

_____

_____

_____

_____

_____

—♥—♥—♥—♥—♥—♥

DAY 120   **DATE:** _____

Describe a dream you've had.

_____

_____

_____

_____

_____

_____

DAY 121 🖤   DATE: _____

If you could create a new law, what would it be?

_____

_____

_____

_____

_____

─★─★─★─★─★─★

DAY 122   DATE: _____

Invent a new pet. What does it look like?

_____

_____

_____

_____

_____

─♥─♥─♥─♥─♥─♥

DAY 123   DATE: _____

What is your favorite thing to do online?

_____

_____

_____

_____

_____

_____

DAY 124 ♥   **DATE:** _____

Describe a place that always makes you happy.

_____

_____

_____

_____

_____

—★—★—★—★—★—★

DAY 125   **DATE:** _____

Write about a time you surprised yourself.

_____

_____

_____

_____

—♥—♥—♥—♥—♥—♥

DAY 126   **DATE:** _____

What do you like best about your family?

_____

_____

_____

_____

_____

DAY 127 ♥   **DATE:** _____

What is the best way to have a perfect day?

_____

_____

_____

_____

_____

—★—★—★—★—★—★

DAY 128   **DATE:** _____

What is your favorite kind of music?

_____

_____

_____

_____

_____

—♥—♥—♥—♥—♥—♥

DAY 129   **DATE:** _____

What do you look forward to about the future?

_____

_____

_____

_____

_____

DAY 130 💙   DATE: _____

What makes you feel nervous? Why?

_____
_____
_____
_____
_____

–★ –★ –★ –★ –★ –★

DAY 131   DATE: _____

How would your friends describe you?

_____
_____
_____
_____
_____

–♥ –♥ –♥ –♥ –♥ –♥

DAY 132   DATE: _____

Who would you want to be stranded on an island with?

_____
_____
_____
_____
_____
_____

DAY 133 🖤   **DATE:** _____

Have you ever had a nickname? If not, come up with one!

_____

_____

_____

_____

_____

— ★ — ★ — ★ — ★ — ★ — ★

DAY 134   **DATE:** _____

Do you like or dislike surprises? Explain why or why not.

_____

_____

_____

_____

_____

— ♥ — ♥ — ♥ — ♥ — ♥ — ♥

DAY 135   **DATE:** _____

What is the bravest thing you've ever done?

_____

_____

_____

_____

_____

DAY 136 ♥   DATE: _____

What is your favorite activity to do on weekends?

_____

_____

_____

_____

_____

—★—★—★—★—★—★

DAY 137   DATE: _____

What kind of clothes or outfits do you like best? Why?

_____

_____

_____

_____

_____

—♥—♥—♥—♥—♥—♥

DAY 138   DATE: _____

If you could jump into a movie, which one would it be?

_____

_____

_____

_____

_____

DAY 139 ♥   DATE: _____

What is something you want to get better at this year?

_____
_____
_____
_____
_____

—★—★—★—★—★—★

DAY 140   DATE: _____

Who do you go to when you need help?

_____
_____
_____
_____
_____

—♥—♥—♥—♥—♥—♥

DAY 141   DATE: _____

What was the best part of your day yesterday?

_____
_____
_____
_____
_____

DAY 142 ♥   **DATE:** _____

Write about a day you never want to forget.

_____

_____

_____

_____

_____

—★—★—★—★—★—★

DAY 143   **DATE:** _____

Five years from now, you will be...

_____

_____

_____

_____

_____

—♥—♥—♥—♥—♥—♥

DAY 144   **DATE:** _____

Name 2 goals you have for yourself.

_____

_____

_____

_____

_____

_____

DAY 145 ♥   **DATE:** _____

What is your favorite kind of weather? Why?

_____

_____

_____

_____

_____

—★—★—★—★—★—★

DAY 146   **DATE:** _____

Write about a babysitting experience.

_____

_____

_____

_____

_____

—♥—♥—♥—♥—♥—♥

DAY 147   **DATE:** _____

Write about something you wished for that came true.

_____

_____

_____

_____

_____

DAY 148 ♥   **DATE:** _____

Describe the best concert/event you've ever attended.

_____

_____

_____

_____

_____

—★—★—★—★—★—★

DAY 149   **DATE:** _____

Write about building sandcastles or swimming.

_____

_____

_____

_____

_____

—♥—♥—♥—♥—♥—♥

DAY 150   **DATE:** _____

Write about a time your parents embarassed you.

_____

_____

_____

_____

_____

_____

DAY 151 ❤   **DATE:** _____

Finish this: I really love it when...

_____

_____

_____

_____

_____

—★—★—★—★—★—★

DAY 152   **DATE:** _____

Write about two things your family has taught you.

_____

_____

_____

_____

_____

—❤—❤—❤—❤—❤—❤

DAY 153   **DATE:** _____

What makes you proud to be from your country?

_____

_____

_____

_____

_____

_____

DAY 154 ♥   DATE: _____

Describe one possession that means the most to you.

_____

_____

_____

_____

_____

−★−★−★−★−★−★

DAY 155   DATE: _____

Describe your best personality trait.

_____

_____

_____

_____

_____

−♥−♥−♥−♥−♥−♥

DAY 156   DATE: _____

Write about the worst fight you ever had with a friend.

_____

_____

_____

_____

_____

_____

DAY 157 🖤   **DATE:** _____

What is your definition of "happiness"?

_____

_____

_____

_____

_____

─★─★─★─★─★─★

DAY 158   **DATE:** _____

What type of exercise or physical activity do you like best?

_____

_____

_____

_____

_____

─♥─♥─♥─♥─♥─♥

DAY 159   **DATE:** _____

What is a secret dream that you have?

_____

_____

_____

_____

_____

_____

DAY 160 ♥   DATE: _____

List three things that would make you a better friend.

_____

_____

_____

_____

_____

—★—★—★—★—★—★

DAY 161   DATE: _____

Do you trust yourself to make good decisions?

_____

_____

_____

_____

_____

—♥—♥—♥—♥—♥—♥

DAY 162   DATE: _____

What does "love" mean to you?

_____

_____

_____

_____

_____

_____

DAY 163 ♥   **DATE:** _____

What was the best part of your day?

_____

_____

_____

_____

_____

—★ —★ —★ —★ —★ —★

DAY 164   **DATE:** _____

Say something positive about one family member.

_____

_____

_____

_____

_____

—♥ —♥ —♥ —♥ —♥ —♥

DAY 165   **DATE:** _____

Who is your favorite superhero or villain?

_____

_____

_____

_____

_____

DAY 166 ♥   DATE: _____

Your dream birthday party would be...

_____

_____

_____

_____

_____

— ★ — ★ — ★ — ★ — ★ — ★

DAY 167   DATE: _____

Finish this sentence: I love summer because...

_____

_____

_____

_____

_____

— ♥ — ♥ — ♥ — ♥ — ♥ — ♥

DAY 168   DATE: _____

Finish this sentence: If I found a pot of gold, I would...

_____

_____

_____

_____

_____

DAY 169 ♥   DATE: _____

Would you rather be able to fly or breathe under water?

_____

_____

_____

_____

_____

—★ —★ —★ —★ —★ —★

DAY 170   DATE: _____

Describe an event that changed your life.

_____

_____

_____

_____

_____

—♥ —♥ —♥ —♥ —♥ —♥

DAY 171   DATE: _____

What is going well in your life right now?

_____

_____

_____

_____

_____

DAY 172 🖤   DATE: _____

What can you do today to take care of yourself?

_____

_____

_____

_____

_____

—★—★—★—★—★—★

DAY 173   DATE: _____

What do you regret the most?

_____

_____

_____

_____

_____

—♥—♥—♥—♥—♥—♥

DAY 174   DATE: _____

Would you want to live forever? Why or why not?

_____

_____

_____

_____

_____

DAY 175 ♥   **DATE:** _____

What is something you're excited about?

_____

_____

_____

_____

_____

—★—★—★—★—★—★

DAY 176   **DATE:** _____

What makes you lost track of time?

_____

_____

_____

_____

_____

—♥—♥—♥—♥—♥—♥

DAY 177   **DATE:** _____

Finish this: My life wouldn't be complete without...

_____

_____

_____

_____

_____

_____

DAY 178 ♥   DATE: _____

Write about an experience standing up for someone.

_____

_____

_____

_____

_____

—★ —★ —★ —★ —★ —★

DAY 179   DATE: _____

Have you ever been bullied or met a bully? Explain.

_____

_____

_____

_____

_____

—♥ —♥ —♥ —♥ —♥ —♥

DAY 180   DATE: _____

Have you ever had an imaginary friend?

_____

_____

_____

_____

_____

DAY 181 ♥   **DATE:** _____

What would you like to invent?

_____

_____

_____

_____

_____

—★ —★ —★ —★ —★ —★

DAY 182   **DATE:** _____

Have you ever broken something? What happened?

_____

_____

_____

_____

_____

—♥ —♥ —♥ —♥ —♥ —♥

DAY 183   **DATE:** _____

What do you like about how you look?

_____

_____

_____

_____

_____

DAY 184 ♥   **DATE:** _____

How do you feel about talking in front of people?

_____

_____

_____

_____

_____

— ★ — ★ — ★ — ★ — ★ — ★

DAY 185   **DATE:** _____

Finish this. Once I rode a unicorn to school and...

_____

_____

_____

_____

_____

— ♥ — ♥ — ♥ — ♥ — ♥ — ♥

DAY 186   **DATE:** _____

Describe a beautiful sunset.

_____

_____

_____

_____

_____

_____

DAY 187 ♥   DATE: _____

What is a rule you think is unfair?

_____
_____
_____
_____
_____

─★─★─★─★─★─★

DAY 188   DATE: _____

Finish this: The one thing that makes me angry is...

_____
_____
_____
_____
_____

─♥─♥─♥─♥─♥─♥

DAY 189   DATE: _____

Write a poem about your family.

_____
_____
_____
_____
_____
_____

DAY 190 ♥   **DATE:** _____

What would you change about where you live?

_____

_____

_____

_____

_____

—★—★—★—★—★—★

DAY 191   **DATE:** _____

What is your favorite thing about where you live?

_____

_____

_____

_____

_____

—♥—♥—♥—♥—♥—♥

DAY 192   **DATE:** _____

List 4 true sentences that begin with: "I remember..."

_____

_____

_____

_____

_____

DAY 193 🖤   **DATE:** _____

What is your favorite outdoor fall activity?

_____

_____

_____

_____

_____

—★—★—★—★—★—★

DAY 194   **DATE:** _____

If you designed a rollercoaster, what would you call it?

_____

_____

_____

_____

_____

—♥—♥—♥—♥—♥—♥

DAY 195   **DATE:** _____

What is the most interesting thing you've ever done?

_____

_____

_____

_____

_____

DAY 196 ♥   **DATE:** _____

Why do you think it's important to love yourself?

_____

_____

_____

_____

_____

— ★ — ★ — ★ — ★ — ★ — ★

DAY 197   **DATE:** _____

Describe something you can't do yet.

_____

_____

_____

_____

_____

— ♥ — ♥ — ♥ — ♥ — ♥ — ♥

DAY 198   **DATE:** _____

What do you like most about your school?

_____

_____

_____

_____

_____

DAY 199 ♥   DATE: _____

Write about a time you felt guilty about something.

_____
_____
_____
_____
_____

—★—★—★—★—★—★

DAY 200   DATE: _____

Imagine being invisible for a day. What would you do?

_____
_____
_____
_____
_____

—♥—♥—♥—♥—♥—♥

DAY 201   DATE: _____

Write what you see when you look in the mirror.

_____
_____
_____
_____
_____
_____

DAY 202 ♥   DATE: _____

Describe one of the greatest lessons you've learned.

_____

_____

_____

_____

_____

—★ —★ —★ —★ —★ —★

DAY 203   DATE: _____

What is the hardest thing about being your age?

_____

_____

_____

_____

_____

—♥—♥—♥—♥—♥—♥

DAY 204   DATE: _____

Who inspired you today?

_____

_____

_____

_____

_____

_____

DAY 205 ♥   DATE: _____

What's the strangest thing you've ever done?

_____
_____
_____
_____
_____

—★ —★ —★ —★ —★ —★

DAY 206   DATE: _____

What do you think your first job will be?

_____
_____
_____
_____
_____

—♥ —♥ —♥ —♥ —♥ —♥

DAY 207   DATE: _____

How would you like to change the world?

_____
_____
_____
_____
_____

DAY 208 ♥   DATE: _____

Do you wish the Internet didn't exist? Why or why not?

_____
_____
_____
_____
_____

—★—★—★—★—★—★

DAY 209   DATE: _____

Have you ever cried watching a movie? Explain.

_____
_____
_____
_____
_____

—♥—♥—♥—♥—♥—♥

DAY 210   DATE: _____

What would you say to someone you miss?

_____
_____
_____
_____
_____

DAY 211 ♥   **DATE:** _____

How does your family make you feel loved?

_____

_____

_____

_____

_____

—★—★—★—★—★—★

DAY 212   **DATE:** _____

What is something you do very well?

_____

_____

_____

_____

_____

—♥—♥—♥—♥—♥—♥

DAY 213   **DATE:** _____

What is your biggest obstacle in school?

_____

_____

_____

_____

_____

_____

DAY 214 ♥   **DATE:** _____

How do you show respect to your parents?

_____

_____

_____

_____

_____

— ★ — ★ — ★ — ★ — ★ — ★

DAY 215   **DATE:** _____

Do you need to apologize to someone? If so, who?

_____

_____

_____

_____

_____

— ♥ — ♥ — ♥ — ♥ — ♥ — ♥

DAY 216   **DATE:** _____

Do you consider yourself a funny person?

_____

_____

_____

_____

_____

_____

DAY 217 ♥   **DATE:** _____

Is being "cool" important to you? Why or why not?

_____

_____

_____

_____

_____

—★—★—★—★—★—★

DAY 218   **DATE:** _____

What makes you proud of your parents?

_____

_____

_____

_____

_____

—♥—♥—♥—♥—♥—♥

DAY 219   **DATE:** _____

What is something nice you could do for someone today?

_____

_____

_____

_____

_____

_____

DAY 220 ♥   DATE: _____

What do you love about yourself?

_____

_____

_____

_____

_____

—★ —★ —★ —★ —★ —★

DAY 221   DATE: _____

When was a time you felt at your absolute best?

_____

_____

_____

_____

_____

—♥ —♥ —♥ —♥ —♥ —♥

DAY 222   DATE: _____

Do you daydream? If so, what about? If not, why not?

_____

_____

_____

_____

_____

_____

DAY 223 ♥   **DATE:** _____

When was a time you felt lucky?

_____

_____

_____

_____

_____

—★—★—★—★—★—★

DAY 224   **DATE:** _____

What is the best gift you've given someone?

_____

_____

_____

_____

_____

—♥—♥—♥—♥—♥—♥

DAY 225   **DATE:** _____

What was your high of the week? Your low?

_____

_____

_____

_____

_____

_____

DAY 226 ♥   DATE: _____

How would you spend the day if you could do anything?

_____

_____

_____

_____

_____

— ★ — ★ — ★ — ★ — ★ — ★

DAY 227   DATE: _____

What is a new habit you'd like to develop?

_____

_____

_____

_____

_____

— ♥ — ♥ — ♥ — ♥ — ♥ — ♥

DAY 228   DATE: _____

What hardships did you experience last school year?

_____

_____

_____

_____

_____

_____

DAY 229 ♥   DATE: _____

Who is your favorite teacher? Why?

_____

_____

_____

_____

_____

—★—★—★—★—★—★

DAY 230   DATE: _____

Write down a promise to yourself.

_____

_____

_____

_____

_____

—♥—♥—♥—♥—♥—♥

DAY 231   DATE: _____

What is your favorite dessert? Why?

_____

_____

_____

_____

_____

_____

DAY 232 ♥   DATE: _____

What is your favorite family activity?

_____

_____

_____

_____

_____

—★—★—★—★—★—★

DAY 233   DATE: _____

How could you improve your relationship with your family?

_____

_____

_____

_____

_____

—♥—♥—♥—♥—♥—♥

DAY 234   DATE: _____

What makes you feel unloved?

_____

_____

_____

_____

_____

_____

DAY 235 ♥   **DATE:** _____

What makes someone lazy?

_____

_____

_____

_____

_____

— ★ — ★ — ★ — ★ — ★ — ★

DAY 236   **DATE:** _____

What healthy things do you do?

_____

_____

_____

_____

_____

— ♥ — ♥ — ♥ — ♥ — ♥ — ♥

DAY 237   **DATE:** _____

When you're frustrated, what do you do?

_____

_____

_____

_____

_____

_____

DAY 238 ♥   **DATE:** _____

What makes you feel confident? Not confident?

_____

_____

_____

_____

_____

—★—★—★—★—★—★

DAY 239   **DATE:** _____

What do you look forward to doing in the years to come?

_____

_____

_____

_____

_____

—♥—♥—♥—♥—♥—♥

DAY 240   **DATE:** _____

What dreams do you have for your family?

_____

_____

_____

_____

_____

DAY 241 🖤   **DATE:** _____

What skills do you have that you can teach others?

_____

_____

_____

_____

_____

—★ —★ —★ —★ —★ —★

DAY 242   **DATE:** _____

What do you think is the meaning of your life?

_____

_____

_____

_____

_____

—♥ —♥ —♥ —♥ —♥ —♥

DAY 243   **DATE:** _____

What five words best describes your life right now?

_____

_____

_____

_____

_____

_____

DAY 244 ♥   **DATE:** _____

How would you describe your parents?

_____

_____

_____

_____

_____

—★—★—★—★—★—★

DAY 245   **DATE:** _____

What is the hardest thing you have had to do this year?

_____

_____

_____

_____

_____

—♥—♥—♥—♥—♥—♥

DAY 246   **DATE:** _____

If you had a pet unicorn, what would you name it?

_____

_____

_____

_____

_____

DAY 247 💗   **DATE:** _____

What type of sounds do you like?

_____

_____

_____

_____

_____

—★—★—★—★—★—★

DAY 248   **DATE:** _____

If you could grow anything in your backyard, what would it be?

_____

_____

_____

_____

_____

—♥—♥—♥—♥—♥—♥

DAY 249   **DATE:** _____

If you wrote a book, what would you call it?

_____

_____

_____

_____

_____

DAY 250 💙   DATE: _____

Would you rather predict the future or read minds?

_____

_____

_____

_____

_____

─★─★─★─★─★─★

DAY 251   DATE: _____

If you could make a new animal, what would it look like?

_____

_____

_____

_____

_____

─❤─❤─❤─❤─❤─❤

DAY 252   DATE: _____

Who is someone in history you would want to meet?

_____

_____

_____

_____

_____

_____

DAY 253 ❤️   DATE: _____

What is your favorite song?

_____

_____

_____

_____

_____

—★—★—★—★—★—★

DAY 254   DATE: _____

If you played hide & go seek today, where would you hide?

_____

_____

_____

_____

_____

—❤—❤—❤—❤—❤—❤

DAY 255   DATE: _____

Do you have a favorite flower?

_____

_____

_____

_____

_____

_____

DAY 256 ♥   DATE: _____

What is the worst thing you've ever eaten?

_____
_____
_____
_____
_____

—★—★—★—★—★—★

DAY 257   DATE: _____

What is your favorite word?

_____
_____
_____
_____
_____

—♥—♥—♥—♥—♥—♥

DAY 258   DATE: _____

Would you rather live back in time or in the future?

_____
_____
_____
_____
_____

DAY 259 ♥   **DATE:** _____

Would you rather be a bird or a fish?

_____

_____

_____

_____

_____

—★ —★ —★ —★ —★ —★

DAY 260   **DATE:** _____

Which musical instrument would you want to play?

_____

_____

_____

_____

_____

—♥—♥—♥—♥—♥—♥

DAY 261   **DATE:** _____

What do you think is the worst chore?

_____

_____

_____

_____

_____

DAY 262 🖤   DATE: _____

If you could talk to an animal, what would you ask?

_____

_____

_____

_____

_____

—★—★—★—★—★—★

DAY 263   DATE: _____

If you opened a store, what would you sell?

_____

_____

_____

_____

_____

—♥—♥—♥—♥—♥—♥

DAY 264   DATE: _____

If you could create a new holiday, what would it be?

_____

_____

_____

_____

_____

DAY 265 🖤   **DATE:** _____

How do you show people you care about them?

_____

_____

_____

_____

_____

–★–★–★–★–★–★

DAY 266   **DATE:** _____

What makes you feel thankful

_____

_____

_____

_____

_____

–♥–♥–♥–♥–♥–♥

DAY 267   **DATE:** _____

What are two things you want to do this summer?

_____

_____

_____

_____

_____

DAY 268 ♥   **DATE:** _____

Are you good at keeping secrets?

_____

_____

_____

_____

_____

—★ —★ —★ —★ —★ —★

DAY 269   **DATE:** _____

Would you rather be a fast swimmer or fast runner?

_____

_____

_____

_____

_____

—♥—♥—♥—♥—♥—♥

DAY 270   **DATE:** _____

Describe your perfect summer day?

_____

_____

_____

_____

_____

DAY 271 🖤   **DATE:** _____

Name one way you could help the environment.

_____
_____
_____
_____
_____

—★ —★ —★ —★ —★ —★

DAY 272   **DATE:** _____

If you were given a shopping spree, what would you buy?

_____
_____
_____
_____
_____

—♥ —♥ —♥ —♥ —♥ —♥

DAY 273   **DATE:** _____

Pretend you're a chef. What would you cook?

_____
_____
_____
_____
_____
_____

DAY 274 ♥   **DATE:** _____

What are some of the best things about nature?

_____
_____
_____
_____
_____

—★—★—★—★—★—★

DAY 275   **DATE:** _____

If you could be any age, what would it be?

_____
_____
_____
_____
_____

—♥—♥—♥—♥—♥—♥

DAY 276   **DATE:** _____

What is your favorite joke?

_____
_____
_____
_____
_____
_____

DAY 277 ♥   **DATE:** _____

What job would you never want to have?

_____

_____

_____

_____

_____

—★—★—★—★—★—★

DAY 278   **DATE:** _____

A gift box appears. What do you hope is inside?

_____

_____

_____

_____

_____

—♥—♥—♥—♥—♥—♥

DAY 279   **DATE:** _____

Do you believe in ghosts? Why or why not?

_____

_____

_____

_____

_____

_____

DAY 280 ♥   **DATE:** _____

What's the craziest thing you've ever done?

_____

_____

_____

_____

_____

— ★ — ★ — ★ — ★ — ★ — ★

DAY 281   **DATE:** _____

Who is your worst enemy and why?

_____

_____

_____

_____

_____

— ♥ — ♥ — ♥ — ♥ — ♥ — ♥

DAY 282   **DATE:** _____

Can you impersonate someone? If so, who?

_____

_____

_____

_____

_____

DAY 283 ♥   **DATE:** _____

Who is your favorite fictional character?

_____

_____

_____

_____

_____

—★ —★ —★ —★ —★ —★

DAY 284   **DATE:** _____

What would your superhero name be?

_____

_____

_____

_____

_____

—♥ —♥ —♥ —♥ —♥ —♥

DAY 285   **DATE:** _____

Would you rather be a snake or a spider?

_____

_____

_____

_____

_____

DAY 286 ♥   DATE: _____

Can you name ten different emotions?

_____

_____

_____

_____

_____

–★ –★ –★ –★ –★ –★

DAY 287   DATE: _____

What would you name a new color?

_____

_____

_____

_____

_____

–♥ –♥ –♥ –♥ –♥ –♥

DAY 288   DATE: _____

What do you love to learn about?

_____

_____

_____

_____

_____

DAY 289 🖤   DATE: _____

What is one fruit or vegetable you wish didn't exist?

_____

_____

_____

_____

_____

—★—★—★—★—★—★

DAY 290   DATE: _____

What's the weirdest thing you've ever seen?

_____

_____

_____

_____

_____

—🖤—🖤—🖤—🖤—🖤—🖤

DAY 291   DATE: _____

If you had a secret hideout, what would be in it?

_____

_____

_____

_____

_____

_____

DAY 292 ♥   DATE: _____

When do you feel jealous of your friends?

_____
_____
_____
_____
_____

—★—★—★—★—★—★

DAY 293   DATE: _____

Describe the house you want to buy when you're older.

_____
_____
_____
_____
_____

—♥—♥—♥—♥—♥—♥

DAY 294   DATE: _____

Would you rather be able to freeze time or speed it up?

_____
_____
_____
_____
_____

DAY 295 ♥   DATE: _____

Describe a time you got hurt.

_____

_____

_____

_____

_____

─★─★─★─★─★─★

DAY 296   DATE: _____

Do you think boys or girls have it easier? Explain?

_____

_____

_____

_____

_____

─♥─♥─♥─♥─♥─♥

DAY 297   DATE: _____

What is your favorite thing to eat for lunch?

_____

_____

_____

_____

_____

DAY 298 ♥   DATE: _____

How are you and your Mom different?

_____

_____

_____

_____

_____

—★—★—★—★—★—★

DAY 299   DATE: _____

How are you and your Mom the same?

_____

_____

_____

_____

_____

—♥—♥—♥—♥—♥—♥

DAY 300   DATE: _____

What is the most important thing your Mom taught you?

_____

_____

_____

_____

_____

_____

DAY 301 🖤   DATE: _____

What was the best holiday you ever had?

_____

_____

_____

_____

_____

—★ —★ —★ —★ —★ —★

DAY 302   DATE: _____

What was the coolest thing you've ever built?

_____

_____

_____

_____

_____

—♥—♥—♥—♥—♥—♥

DAY 303   DATE: _____

What's something you don't like about winter?

_____

_____

_____

_____

_____

DAY 304 ♥   **DATE:** _____

What color is the "happiest color" to you?

_____

_____

_____

_____

_____

—★—★—★—★—★—★

DAY 305   **DATE:** _____

How can people tell when you're happy?

_____

_____

_____

_____

_____

—♥—♥—♥—♥—♥—♥

DAY 306   **DATE:** _____

What is your favorite candy?

_____

_____

_____

_____

_____

DAY 307 ♥   DATE: _____

What is your favorite room in the house? Why?

_____
_____
_____
_____
_____

—★—★—★—★—★—★

DAY 308   DATE: _____

What do you think it beyond the stars?

_____
_____
_____
_____
_____

—♥—♥—♥—♥—♥—♥

DAY 309   DATE: _____

Would you rather travel by airplane or by train?

_____
_____
_____
_____
_____
_____

DAY 310 ♥   **DATE:** _____

What's the best thing that's happened to you lately?

_____

_____

_____

_____

_____

─★─★─★─★─★─★

DAY 311   **DATE:** _____

Which one of Snow White's dwarves would you be?

_____

_____

_____

_____

_____

─♥─♥─♥─♥─♥─♥

DAY 312   **DATE:** _____

If you could understand any animal, which would it be?

_____

_____

_____

_____

_____

_____

DAY 313 ♥   **DATE:** _____

What would your superhero costume look like?

_____

_____

_____

_____

_____

—★ —★ —★ —★ —★ —★

DAY 314   **DATE:** _____

If you could pick your own bedtime, when would it be?

_____

_____

_____

_____

_____

—♥—♥—♥—♥—♥—♥

DAY 315   **DATE:** _____

What animal do you think is the coolest? The scariest?

_____

_____

_____

_____

_____

_____

DAY 316 ♥   **DATE:** _____

What is your favorite thing about each season?

_____

_____

_____

_____

_____

—★—★—★—★—★—★

DAY 317   **DATE:** _____

If you could have dinner with anyone, who would it be?

_____

_____

_____

_____

_____

—♥—♥—♥—♥—♥—♥

DAY 318   **DATE:** _____

Who would you most love to prank?

_____

_____

_____

_____

_____

DAY 319 ♥   DATE: _____

What is the scariest movie you've ever seen?

_____

_____

_____

_____

_____

—★—★—★—★—★—★

DAY 320   DATE: _____

What would people be surprised to know about you?

_____

_____

_____

_____

_____

—♥—♥—♥—♥—♥—♥

DAY 321   DATE: _____

If you were an artist, what would you paint?

_____

_____

_____

_____

_____

_____

DAY 322 ♥   DATE: _____

Do you have any phobias? If so, what are they?

_____

_____

_____

_____

_____

—★—★—★—★—★—★

DAY 323   DATE: _____

If you could change one family rule, what would it be?

_____

_____

_____

_____

_____

—♥—♥—♥—♥—♥—♥

DAY 324   DATE: _____

What are three things that you do every day?

_____

_____

_____

_____

_____

DAY 325 🖤   **DATE:** _____

Where is your favorite place in the world?

_____

_____

_____

_____

_____

—★—★—★—★—★—★

DAY 326   **DATE:** _____

What is something you do that bothers other people?

_____

_____

_____

_____

_____

—♥—♥—♥—♥—♥—♥

DAY 327   **DATE:** _____

What is happening in the world that bothers you?

_____

_____

_____

_____

_____

_____

DAY 328 ♥   **DATE:** _____

Are you an organized person or messy?

_____

_____

_____

_____

_____

— ★ — ★ — ★ — ★ — ★ — ★

DAY 329   **DATE:** _____

What is the best kind of food for a food fight?

_____

_____

_____

_____

_____

— ♥ — ♥ — ♥ — ♥ — ♥ — ♥

DAY 330   **DATE:** _____

Tell me about your perfect pizza.

_____

_____

_____

_____

_____

DAY 331 🖤   DATE: _____

Describe the perfect ice cream sundae.

_____

_____

_____

_____

_____

—★—★—★—★—★—★

DAY 332   DATE: _____

Can you say the alphabet backwards? Give it a try!

_____

_____

_____

_____

_____

—♥—♥—♥—♥—♥—♥

DAY 333   DATE: _____

Who would you like to have a snowball fight with?

_____

_____

_____

_____

_____

DAY 334 ♥   DATE: _____

Would you rather always wake up early or go to bed late?

_____

_____

_____

_____

_____

–★–★–★–★–★–★

DAY 335   DATE: _____

If you could teach a dog a new trick, what would it be?

_____

_____

_____

_____

_____

–♥–♥–♥–♥–♥–♥

DAY 336   DATE: _____

What would be the worst animal to have as a pet?

_____

_____

_____

_____

_____

DAY 337 ♥   DATE: _____

What makes someone smart?

_____

_____

_____

_____

_____

−★−★−★−★−★−★

DAY 338   DATE: _____

What is a secret you haven't told anyone?

_____

_____

_____

_____

_____

−♥−♥−♥−♥−♥−♥

DAY 339   DATE: _____

What do you want to learn how to do?

_____

_____

_____

_____

_____

DAY 340 💙   DATE: _____

What do you think about when you are bored?

_____

_____

_____

_____

_____

—★—★—★—★—★—★

DAY 341   DATE: _____

What is the most boring part of school?

_____

_____

_____

_____

_____

—♥—♥—♥—♥—♥—♥

DAY 342   DATE: _____

What is your favorite thing to drink?

_____

_____

_____

_____

_____

DAY 343 🖤   DATE: _____

What animal are you most afraid of?

_____

_____

_____

_____

_____

—★ —★ —★ —★ —★ —★

DAY 344   DATE: _____

If you could make it one season all year, which would it be?

_____

_____

_____

_____

_____

—♥—♥—♥—♥—♥—♥

DAY 345   DATE: _____

What is your favorite breakfast food?

_____

_____

_____

_____

_____

DAY 346 ♥   **DATE:** _____

What is your favorite flower or plant?

_____

_____

_____

_____

_____

—★ —★ —★ —★ —★ —★

DAY 347   **DATE:** _____

What would the world be like with kids in charge?

_____

_____

_____

_____

_____

—♥—♥—♥—♥—♥—♥

DAY 348   **DATE:** _____

Tell me about a time when you did something creative.

_____

_____

_____

_____

_____

DAY 349 ♥   DATE: _____

Tell me about a time when you forgave someone.

_____

_____

_____

_____

_____

—★ —★ —★ —★ —★ —★

DAY 350   DATE: _____

Tell me about a time when you made a mistake.

_____

_____

_____

_____

_____

—♥—♥—♥—♥—♥—♥

DAY 351   DATE: _____

Who is your favorite aunt or uncle? Why?

_____

_____

_____

_____

_____

_____

DAY 352 ♥   **DATE:** _____

What is your favorite restaurant?

_____

_____

_____

_____

_____

★ — ★ — ★ — ★ — ★ — ★

DAY 353   **DATE:** _____

Tell me how it feels when someone compliments you.

_____

_____

_____

_____

_____

♥ — ♥ — ♥ — ♥ — ♥ — ♥

DAY 354   **DATE:** _____

If you were stuck on an island what three things would you bring with you?

_____

_____

_____

_____

_____

DAY 355 ♥   **DATE:** _____

Would you ever go skydiving?

_____

_____

_____

_____

_____

—★ —★ —★ —★ —★ —★

DAY 356   **DATE:** _____

What was the high point and low point of your day?

_____

_____

_____

_____

_____

—♥—♥—♥—♥—♥—♥

DAY 357   **DATE:** _____

What's your biggest challenge right now?

_____

_____

_____

_____

_____

DAY 358 ♥   DATE: _____

What are three things you are grateful for right now?

_____

_____

_____

_____

_____

—★ —★ —★ —★ —★ —★

DAY 359   DATE: _____

Would you rather live in the city or country? Why?

_____

_____

_____

_____

_____

—♥—♥—♥—♥—♥—♥

DAY 360   DATE: _____

What is the funniest word you know?

_____

_____

_____

_____

_____

DAY 361 ♥   **DATE:** _____

If you could give everyone in your family new names,
what would they be?

_____

_____

_____

_____

─★─★─★─★─★─★

DAY 362   **DATE:** _____

Who is the nicest person you know?

_____

_____

_____

_____

_____

─♥─♥─♥─♥─♥─♥

DAY 363   **DATE:** _____

What makes you feel special?

_____

_____

_____

_____

_____

_____

DAY 364 ♥   **DATE:** _____

When do you feel happiest?

_____

_____

_____

_____

_____

–★–★–★–★–★–★

DAY 365   **DATE:** _____

What made you smile today? ☺

_____

_____

_____

_____

_____

–♥–♥–♥–♥–♥–♥

Congrats!
You completed the journal!

Made in the USA
Columbia, SC
17 December 2022

74427588R00072